Do People Really Have Tiny Insects Living in Their Eyelashes?

And Other Questions about the Microscopic World

MELISSA STEWART

ILLUSTRATIONS BY COLIN W. THOMPSON

LERNER PUBLICATIONS COMPANY

Minneapolis

Contents

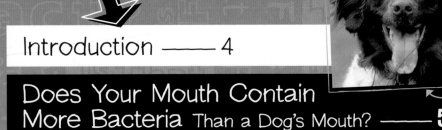

Perhaps you've heard these common beliefs about the microscopic world:

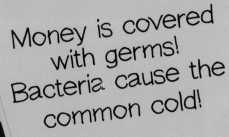

Money is covered with germs! Bacteria cause the common cold!

But are these things true?

Is there any science behind them? Come along with us as we explore these old beliefs and more. Find out whether the stories and sayings you've heard about the microscopic world are

FACT OR FICTION!

Does Your Mouth Contain More Bacteria Than a Dog's Mouth?

MAYBE. It depends on the size of the dog.

Here's a better question: whose mouth has more bacteria per square inch—a person's or a dog's? That question is much easier to answer. It's pretty much a tie.

Your mouth is wet and warm. It's full of tiny bits of food. That makes it the perfect place for bacteria to live and grow. A dog's mouth is no different.

At any moment, fifty billion bacteria could be living inside your mouth. There are other kinds of germs too. A dog with the same size mouth would have about the same number of itty-bitty invaders.

Why do some people think a human mouth is dirtier than a dog's? Because the wound from a human bite is more likely to get infected than the wound from a dog bite. But that's because many of the germs in a dog's mouth only affect dogs. They can make another dog sick, but they can't harm a person.

Do Most People Really Have Tiny Insects Living in Their Eyelashes?

NO. But that doesn't mean your lashes are free of creepy crawlies.

An eyelash mite on human skin

Insects such as this grasshopper have three body parts.

An insect has three body parts—a head, a thorax, and an abdomen. It also has six legs. Butterflies and beetles are insects. But critters such as mites are not. And it's pretty common for mites to make themselves at home on people's eyelashes. In fact, believe it or not, most people's eyelashes contain mites.

Eyelash mites have two body parts and eight legs. They belong to the same group of animals as spiders and ticks. Eyelash mites look like tiny worms. A dozen eyelash mites could easily fit on the head of a pin. They have stumpy legs with tiny claws. They spend their days sucking on juices that ooze out of your skin. Sometimes they munch on dead skin cells too.

Eyelash mites often spend their whole lives on a person's eyelashes. Whenever you blink, they go along for the ride. Just think about it: That means these little creatures bounce up and down more than ten thousand times a day!

A female eyelash mite lays up to twenty-five eggs at once. The young mites grow quickly. In about two weeks, they are ready to lay eggs of their own.

Most of the time, you don't notice eyelash mites. But if you don't wash your face much, they can start to pile up. Then your eyelashes may fall out sooner than they normally would.

Did You Know?

Not all eyelash mites live on eyelashes. Sometimes they like to hang out on a person's nose, forehead, cheeks, or chin.

Is It True That Tiny Creatures Make Your Skin Itch?

THEY CAN SOMETIMES. Once in a while, people itch when tiny mites dig into their skin. Itch mites are about six times larger than eyelash mites. But they're still too small to see.

Itch mites only live on humans, and they often spread from person to person. All it takes is a quick handshake. Luckily, itch mites are less common than their eyelash-dwelling cousins. Only about 2 percent of North Americans have them.

A male itch mite spends his whole life on a person's skin. He doesn't cause any trouble at all. But the female is a different story. She burrows into skin and builds tunnels more than 1 inch (2.5 centimeters) long. As she digs, she sucks on body juices and lays more than one hundred eggs.

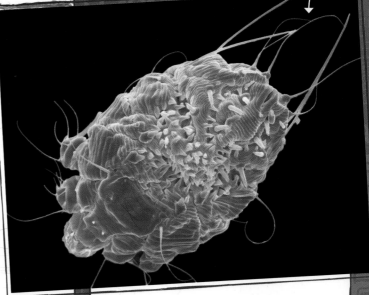

This microscopic image of an itch mite gives a close-up view of the critter. Color was added to the image to help make the dust mite visible.

Chemicals from the female's body cause a rash called scabies. It makes a person's skin red and itchy. Scabies is most common under armpits, on wrists and legs, and between fingers. Getting rid of scabies isn't easy. You'll have to visit a doctor. The doctor can prescribe medicines to ease the itch and kill the mites.

But don't worry too much the next time your skin itches. You probably don't have itch mites. The most likely cause is a bunch of dead skin cells. Your skin is your body's largest organ.

It's made up of billions of cells. All those cells form deep inside your skin. Then they slowly move up to the surface.

By the time the cells reach the top of your skin, they are dead. About fifty thousand of them fall off your body every minute!

Sometimes dead skin cells get stuck. They can't rub off, so they pile up. That's when you start to feel itchy. It's you brain's way of saying, "Scratch off those dead skin cells." And your fingers quickly obey.

Are There Really Millions of Tiny Creatures Living under Your Bed?

YOU BET! Just 1 ounce (28 grams) of dust can contain more than twelve thousand tiny dust mites. If you haven't vacuumed under your bed lately, millions of dust mites could be down there.

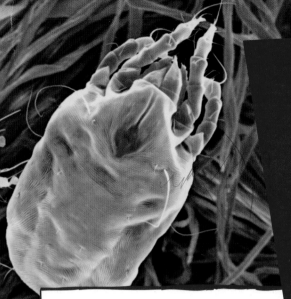

Dangerous Droppings

Dust mites can't make you sick, but their droppings might. A mite makes about twenty waste pellets every day. Some people are allergic to the pellets. These people must keep their carpets and bedding very clean. If they breathe in too many droppings, they could sneeze a lot or get a runny nose. Their eyes will probably get red and puffy. They might even have a hard time breathing.

Dust mites aren't just under your bed. They're in it too. Thousands live in your pillow. Even more make their home on your blankets. And who knows how many dust mites are hiding inside your mattress!

Dust mites live near you, but not on you. That's because they don't feed on liquids from your body. They gobble up the millions of dead skin cells that fall off you every day. An average adult loses a plateful of dead skin cells every year. That's quite a feast for critters one-fifth the size of the head of a pin!

Like other mites, a dust mite lives for just a few months. Females lay forty to eighty eggs. The young hatch in less than a week and grow up quickly.

A dust mite doesn't have jaws or teeth. That means it can't chew its food. When a mite is hungry, it spits juices onto its food. The juices break down dead skin cells. Then the mite sucks up the tasty treat, just like a milk shake through a straw.

Do Bacteria Really Cause the Common Cold?

NO WAY! Bacteria can make you sick, but they don't cause the common cold. You can blame that on viruses. Viruses also cause the flu, chicken pox, warts, and lots of other illnesses.

Bacteria and viruses are both germs—tiny particles or living things that can make you sick. Bacteria are pesky one-celled critters. They cause earaches, food poisoning, Lyme disease, strep throat, and tooth decay. They reproduce by splitting in half, and they come in three shapes—spheres; spirals; and long, thin rods.

Two other types of germs make trouble for humans—protozoa and fungi. Protozoa are small too. But they can move on their own and catch even smaller creatures. Protozoa can cause diseases such as African sleeping sickness and malaria.

Fungi are made of thin threads. As they grow, the threads branch out and take in nutrients. Fungi can cause athlete's foot, food poisoning, and ringworm. Yuck!

Viruses are the smallest germs of all. Five hundred million of them can easily fit on the head of a pin. How can something so small be alive? Well, most scientists say viruses aren't alive. And since they aren't alive, they can't reproduce on their own. They need

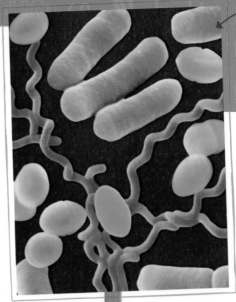

The three common types of bacteria are shown in this microscopic image.

to invade a living thing—like you—and use its cells to reproduce.

When a virus attacks your body, it sneaks into your cells and takes control. It forces your cells to crank out hundreds of new viruses. When a cell is chock-full of viruses, it explodes. The viruses burst out. Then each one invades a new cell.

Believe it or not, more than one hundred kinds of viruses can cause the common cold. And just about every illness you can think of is caused by a germ. Scientists have identified at least five thousand kinds of viruses and thirty thousand kinds of bacteria. There are probably thousands more left to discover.

Did You Know?

You can't catch a cold from a dog or a cat. But you can catch the flu from a whale, a pig, a horse, or a duck.

Is It True That the Germs in a Sneeze Can Travel Only an Arm's Length?

NOPE. Those germs can travel farther than that. Sneezing helps your body get rid of the germs, dirt, and itty-bitty bugs that get sucked into your nose. When these tiny trespassers land inside your nose, warning signals race to your brain. Then a wave of messages rushes to your chest muscles. And the muscles thrust the tiny invaders out of your body with a good, strong "achoo."

That's good news for you, but not for the people around you. A single sneeze can contain enough cold viruses to infect a thousand people.

Each sneeze hurls about forty thousand tiny droplets of spit and mucus out of your nose and mouth. The droplets travel at speeds of 150 miles (241 kilometers) per hour. Scientists have known for a long time that the blasting breath of a sneeze can travel up to 30 feet (9 meters). But nobody thought the wet droplets—or the germs in them—could spray that far. Scientists believed that gravity quickly pulled the heavy drops down to the ground. They thought the germy spray might travel about 3 feet (1 m). But it turns out they were wrong.

In 2007, a team of Australian scientists made an important discovery. They found that the droplets in a sneeze dry very quickly in the air. In fact, the liquid evaporates, or turns into a gas, when the material is just 4 inches (10 cm) from your mouth. Evaporated liquid can travel very far—much farther than an arm's length. This means the germs in the liquid can travel farther than an arm's length too.

So the next time you feel a sneeze coming on, grab a tissue. If you don't have one, sneeze into your sleeve. You'll be doing your family and friends a big favor.

Does Washing Your Hands with Soap and Water Really Get Rid of Germs?

IT SURE DOES!
Washing your hands with soap and warm water is the best way to rinse away germs. And that will help you stay healthy.

Want some proof? When 305 school children in Detroit, Michigan, started washing their hands four times a day, the number of sick days due to colds decreased by 24 percent. Sick days resulting from stomachaches fell by 51 percent.

Germs are on almost everything you touch. After a while, they build up on your hands. They get caught in the folds of skin between your fingers. They also get stuck under your fingernails.

Wash your hands for just 10 seconds, and you'll rinse away about 90 percent of the germs. Wash them for 20 seconds, and almost all the germs will drain down the sink. But don't forget the soap! Washing without it leaves a lot of germs behind. Some people say liquid soap works better than bar soap. But don't believe them. Bar soap works just as well. Other people think antibacterial soap is better than regular soap. The truth is, when you add warm water and make some suds, antibacterial and regular soap are equally good at washing away germs.

When should you wash your hands?
- Before you eat or touch food
- After you go to the bathroom
- After you sneeze or blow your nose
- After you pet an animal

How to Wash

1. Wet your hands with warm water and lather with soap.
2. Rub your hands front and back and between the fingers. Don't forget your fingernails.
3. After about 20 seconds, rinse your hands well. Then dry them with a clean towel.

Is Money Covered with Germs That Can Make You Sick?

YES! Germs are everywhere. They're floating in the air. They're stuck to desks, doorknobs, and TV remote controls. Why should money be any different? After all, think about how many people's hands probably touch a quarter or a one-dollar bill every day. Some of those people are bound to be sick.

Keeping It Clean

In Japan, people can get money from "clean ATMs." These machines press money to flatten out wrinkles (right). Then they heat it to 392°F (200°C). That kills bacteria and other germs.

In 1988, Australia changed its money in a big way. The government started making it out of rubbery plastic instead of paper. The new bills fight off germs. They also last longer. Twenty-two countries have since switched to plastic bills.

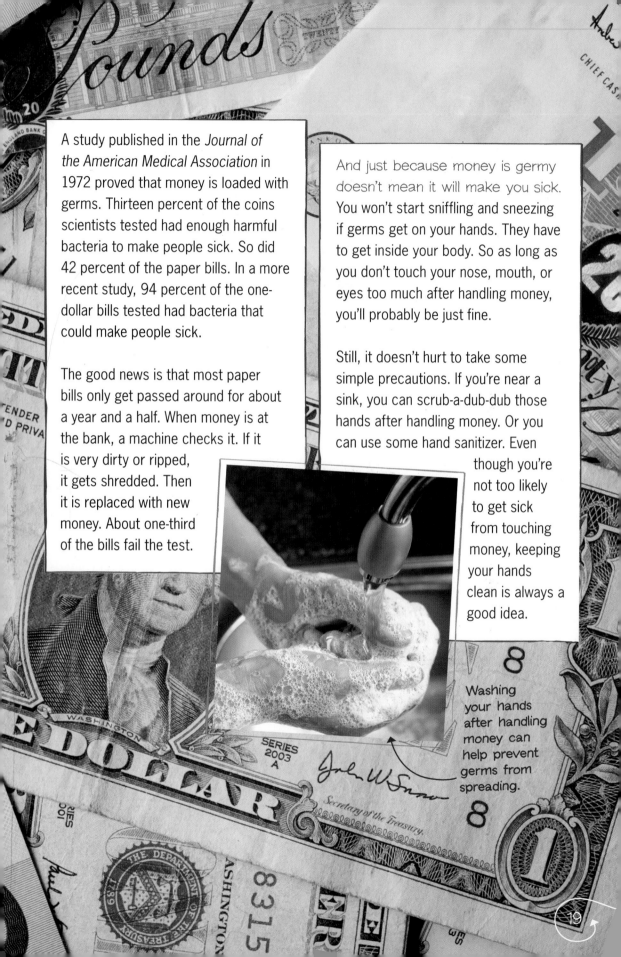

A study published in the *Journal of the American Medical Association* in 1972 proved that money is loaded with germs. Thirteen percent of the coins scientists tested had enough harmful bacteria to make people sick. So did 42 percent of the paper bills. In a more recent study, 94 percent of the one-dollar bills tested had bacteria that could make people sick.

The good news is that most paper bills only get passed around for about a year and a half. When money is at the bank, a machine checks it. If it is very dirty or ripped, it gets shredded. Then it is replaced with new money. About one-third of the bills fail the test.

And just because money is germy doesn't mean it will make you sick. You won't start sniffling and sneezing if germs get on your hands. They have to get inside your body. So as long as you don't touch your nose, mouth, or eyes too much after handling money, you'll probably be just fine.

Still, it doesn't hurt to take some simple precautions. If you're near a sink, you can scrub-a-dub-dub those hands after handling money. Or you can use some hand sanitizer. Even though you're not too likely to get sick from touching money, keeping your hands clean is always a good idea.

Washing your hands after handling money can help prevent germs from spreading.

Is It True That Germs Can Live on Kitchen Sponges?

YOU BET! In fact, most kitchen sponges are loaded with germs.

This image taken through a microscope shows all the germs on a kitchen sponge.

Think about it. Sponges are the perfect home for bacteria and other germs. They're damp and covered with bits of food. All the little holes on the surface of a sponge give the germs lots of places to hide!

Just how germy is a kitchen sponge? One study showed that most sponges have more than 134,000 bacteria per square inch (864,500 per sq. cm). Sound like a lot? It sure is. The same study found that kitchen floors are much cleaner. They have just 830 bacteria per square inch (5,350 per sq. cm). That's a big difference!

Get ready for an even bigger surprise. Kitchen garbage cans have about 400 bacteria per square inch (2,580 per sq. cm). Toilet seats have about 300 bacteria per square inch (1,935 per sq. cm). Can you believe a kitchen sponge is about 450 times germier than a toilet seat?

How does a kitchen sponge get so dirty? Many of the bacteria come from food. The juice from raw meat can be full of germs. So can the skins of fruits and vegetables. Before your slice an apple or cucumber, be sure to wash it. But don't rinse meat. It's better to let its bacteria die when you cook it.

When you clean your kitchen with a sponge, germs from the sponge end up on the counter. Think about that the next time you set a cookie on the counter while you pour a glass of milk. Yuck! No wonder Americans report 76 million cases of food-related sickness every year!

Here's the good news. It's easy to help your kitchen sponge clean up its act. You can soak it in bleach or lemon juice. That kills up to 87 percent of the bacteria. For even better results, put your sponge in a microwave and run it on high power for two minutes. (Make sure your sponge is wet when you put it in the microwave.) You can also kill almost all the germs on a sponge by cleaning it in the dishwasher.

Fluids from raw meat like chicken can be full of germs.

Does Some Water Contain Microbes That Can Kill People?

YES. A microbe is a tiny living thing. Bacteria, fungi, and protozoa are all microbes. Each year, microbes in water kill more than 2 million people around the world. Many more get sick. But people living in such places as the United States, Canada, Western Europe, and Australia don't have to worry. They drink some of the cleanest water in the world.

What makes their water so pure? In most cities and towns, the water doesn't flow straight from a river or lake into homes. It goes to a water treatment plant first. At the plant, water passes through filters that strain out most microbes. Workers add chemicals to kill the tiniest critters. Then scientists test the water to make sure it's safe.

Water treament plants such as this one filter microbes out of drinking water.

In some parts of Asia, Africa, and South America, water is not treated. Sometimes people go to the bathroom in or near the river, the stream, the lake, or the pond where they get drinking water. No wonder so many of them get sick!

You may have heard that bottled water is safer than treated tap water. But it's not. Most bottled water has about the same number of microbes as treated tap water.

Sometimes it has more. It depends on how clean the bottling plant is.

In the United States, Canada, Western Europe, and Australia, the rules for testing tap water are stricter than the rules for testing bottled water. But if your family uses bottled water, that shouldn't bother you too much. You'd be surprised how much bottled water comes straight from the tap!

How can you tell where the water in a bottle comes from? Look at the label. If it says the water is from "a municipal source," or "a community water system," it isn't coming from a fresh mountain stream. Up to 40 percent of the bottled water sold in the United States comes from a tap.

Did You Know?

A glass of water usually contains between one hundred and ten thousand bacteria. But most of them can't make you sick. Some doctors think they may help make your immune system stronger.

Are Microbes Really the Most Deadly Creatures on Earth?

MAYBE, BUT IT'S HARD TO KNOW FOR SURE.
Microbes do kill more people than any other creature. But that's only because humans don't have any natural enemies.

Most creatures have lots of predators, so they're always on the lookout for danger. Lions hunt zebras. Foxes attack rabbits. Snakes catch frogs, and frogs eat flies. The list goes on and on. Even some plants get in on the action. Venus flytraps catch and digest tiny insects. Which of these creatures is the most deadly of all? It's impossible to say.

Humans kill other creatures too. In the United States, people chow down on 15 billion hamburgers every year. The hamburger meat comes from cattle. People also dine on fish, chickens, turkeys, and pigs. The nutrients in these meats help us live and grow.

Most animals use their teeth to catch prey. But people have learned to build all kinds of weapons. Sometimes we use them on other animals. And unfortunately, sometimes we use them on one another.

Foxes *(above)* and venus flytraps *(opposite page)* are both deadly predators.

During the U.S. Civil War (1861–1865), about two hundred thousand soldiers were killed in battle. More than four hundred thousand died later. They had wounds that were infected by germs.

In every war fought before the mid-1900s, microbes killed more people than guns or swords. Why can microbes do so much damage? Because there are lots of them. Some bacteria divide every twenty minutes. In just three days, one cell could produce billions of new microbes. Luckily, our immune systems are always hard at work and usually manage to fight off the harmful ones.

Hundreds of thousands of soldiers died during the U.S. Civil War. Many of them died from wounds infected by germs.

Is It True That Microbes Have Saved Millions of Lives?

IT SURE IS! Some microbes are real troublemakers. They cause such illnesses as Lyme disease and strep throat. They infect cuts and poison our food. But other microbes fight the bad guys. They help us stay healthy.

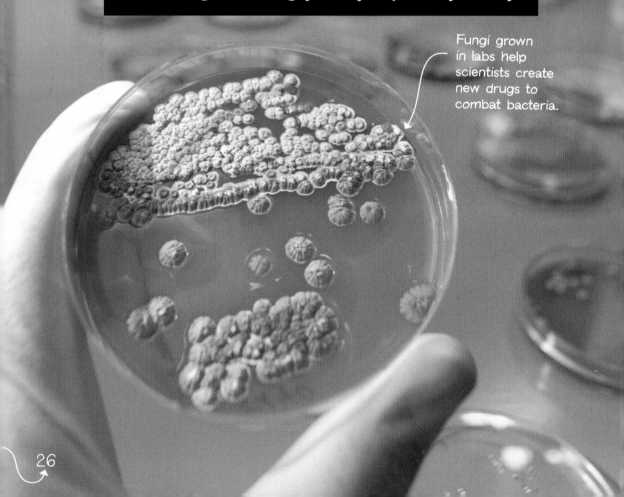

Fungi grown in labs help scientists create new drugs to combat bacteria.

Not long ago, scientists found a soil bacterium that lowers the level of cholesterol in a person's bloodstream. Cholesterol clogs blood vessels and may cause heart disease. Scientists also discovered a fungus that fights breast cancer. The fungus grows naturally on some trees in the American West.

Scientific researchers will probably find more helpful microbes in the next few years. But one of the best discoveries dates back to 1928. That's when a Scottish scientist named Alexander Fleming (below) found a fungus that can kill many kinds of harmful bacteria.

an antibiotic—a medicine that kills bacteria and other microbes.

During World War II (1939-1945), penicillin saved millions of lives. It stopped wounds from getting infected. Penicillin is still used to cure many illnesses caused by bacteria. You might have taken it when you had an earache.

Scientists have also discovered other antibiotics. And it's a good thing too. Bacteria are changing all the time. Some bacteria have changed in ways that protect them from penicillin. That means penicillin can no longer be used to kill them.

Doctors worry that some bacteria might become resistant to all antibiotics. But there are things we can do to stop that from happening. When a doctor gives you an antibiotic, be sure to keep taking it until all the pills are gone. Don't stop when you start to feel better. If you don't take all the pills, some bacteria might be left in your body. They could change and then infect another person. That person wouldn't be able to use the same antibiotic to get healthy.

Scientists thought that if they could grow the fungus in labs, they could make it into a medicine. At first, they had trouble growing large amounts of the fungus. It took them many years to learn how. But once they learned, they could finally make the drug we call penicillin. Penicillin is

Does Your Body Really Contain as Many Bacteria as It Does Human Cells?

ACTUALLY, IT CONTAINS EVEN MORE.
Lots more. Bacteria and other microbes started to move into your body the minute you were born. Germs are in every breath you take. They're in every bit of food you eat. They're on everything you touch too.

This close-up photo shows bacteria in the small intestine.

Bacteria in your intestine help you digest vegetables like broccoli.

Some scientists say that 90 percent of the cells in our bodies are microbes. Millions of these are fungi and protozoa. But even more of them are bacteria. Your insides are crawling with bacteria.

Where are all those bacteria? Mostly in your nose, mouth, and intestines. You breathe in new bacteria every day. Many of them get stuck in your nose hairs. Others get trapped in mucus. But a few land in your throat or lungs, and they can make you sick.

How many bacteria are in your mouth right now? More than seven billion. So far, scientists have studied about four hundred different kinds. Some cause trouble, like tooth decay. But most are harmless. Some are even helpful. These good guys crowd out germs that could make you sick. Some gobble up the bacteria that cause cavities.

Your large intestine has the most bacteria of all. There are more than 100 trillion of them—and that's a good thing. You couldn't live without them. You need bacteria to digest the fruits and vegetables you eat. The bacteria make vitamin K, which helps your blood clot when you get a cut. And bacteria also make B vitamins. B vitamins do many important jobs in your body. They help you get energy from food. They make nerves work better. They also keep your skin, hair, and eyes in tip-top shape.

Vitamins keep you looking healthy.

Did You Know?

Bacteria live on your skin too. Believe it or not, more than 250 bacteria are hanging out on every square inch (1,600 per sq. cm) of your back. About 250,000 live on each square inch (1,613,000 per sq. cm) of your scalp, and about 2.5 million are on each square inch (16.1 million per sq. cm) of your armpits. Like the bacteria inside you, most of the little guys on you cause no harm.

Do Microbes Cause Body Odor and Bad Breath?

YES. Have you ever kicked off your shoes and nearly passed out? Maybe you've sniffed your underarm and then been sorry. What you're smelling are wastes from microbes.

A person's skin has more than two million tiny sweat glands. Every day, they crank out enough sweat to fill a 1-liter (1-quart) soda bottle.

When your body heats up, your sweat glands go into overdrive. On really hot days, they may make more than 2.5 gallons (9.5 liters) of sweat.

That can be bad news because the more you sweat, the more you smell. But don't blame your sweat glands. They're just trying to keep you cool. The real bad guys are bacteria living on your skin.

Some bacteria love dark, damp places, such as armpits and sweaty shoes. They feast on dead skin cells and oils from your skin. The more they eat, the more they grow. Finally, they get so big that they split in half. Then there are twice as many bacteria!

As bacteria multiply, they eat more and more food and produce more and more wastes. And those wastes really reek.

How can you get rid of the terrible stench? It's easy. Take a shower. Soap and water wash away the bacteria. They wash away their food supply and waste products too.

Bacteria on your skin aren't the only stinkers. The ones in your mouth give off their own smelly wastes.

Most of the time, spit does a good job of keeping your mouth clean. That's why some people call it nature's mouthwash. Saliva is full of chemicals that kill bacteria. It also washes away the dead cells and their wastes.

During the day, more than a tablespoon of new saliva floods your mouth every hour. But the flow slows to a trickle while you're asleep. That's why most people have bad breath in the morning. Luckily, it's easy to get rid of the stinky smell. Just brush your teeth.

Brushing your teeth is the best way to get rid of bad breath.

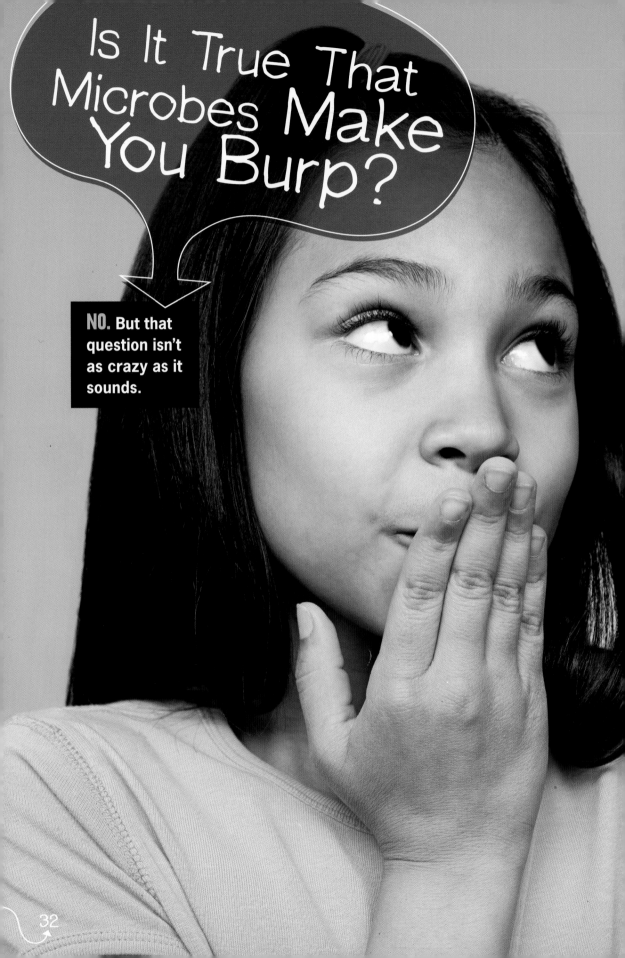

Is It True That Microbes Make You Burp?

NO. But that question isn't as crazy as it sounds.

When you eat, you don't swallow only food. You swallow air too. Most of the time, the air you take in travels to your lungs. But when you eat, a tiny flap blocks the tube that leads to your lungs. That means the air ends up in your stomach. After a while, your stomach can't hold any more air. The air bursts out, races up your throat, and explodes out of your mouth.

Most people burp a few times after they eat. But that's nothing compared to cows. Every year, cattle in North America belch about 50 million tons (45 million metric tons) of gases into the air! And microbes *do* make cows burp.

A cow's body can't digest the grasses it eats. The plants are too tough. Luckily, billions of bacteria live in a cow's four stomachs. As the bacteria feast on the grass, they break it down. They release lots of gases at the same time.

DANGEROUS GAS

Cows also release gases from the "other end" of their bodies—and so do people. Indeed most people pass wind about fourteen times a day!

Where does all that gas come from? It comes from bacteria, just like the gas that makes cows burp. The bacteria live in your intestines. They help your body break down food just as bacteria help cows digest.

Have you ever noticed that foods such as beans, onions, and broccoli can make you gassy? That's because bacteria in your intestines have to work extra hard to break them down.

Did You Know?

Every day, humans produce more than 11 billion pounds (5 billion kilograms) of poop. Up to 65 percent of it is dead bacteria.

Do Some Foods Really Contain Tiny Insect Body Parts?

YEP. Think about it. Have you ever seen an apple with a caterpillar on it? How about lettuce with a few little gnats? Before you ate the food, you probably washed off those tiny critters. But what if you hadn't noticed the insects? You would have eaten them along with your food. Believe it or not, it happens all the time.

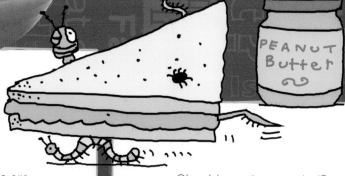

You can't check the apples that go into your applesauce. You can't inspect the peanuts used to make your peanut butter. These crops are picked quickly by people who won't eat them. They might even be picked by machines. Who knows how many bugs go along for the ride? Then machines crush the apples. Other machines grind up the peanuts. The insect hitchhikers get mashed up too, and nobody notices. Most people eat about 2 pounds (1 kg) of insects every year. And they don't even know it.

Should you be worried? Nope. Eating a few insect parts is no big deal. You might even get a little extra protein. But there are limits. The U.S. Food and Drug Administration (FDA) sets guidelines to protect your health. For example, a regular-size chocolate bar can't contain more than thirty-four tiny insect parts, and a jar of tomato sauce can't have more than twenty-two hundred insect eggs or fifteen maggots.

Bug-alicious

In many parts of the world, people think insects are a tasty treat. People eat termites in Ghana, Africa. They fry the insects or add them to bread. In Southeast Asia, some people boil dragonflies in coconut milk. Then they add ginger and garlic. Yum! And in Mexico, people eat agave worms on tortillas.

Is It True That Yogurt Contains Live Bacteria?

SOME BRANDS DO. To make yogurt, workers add two kinds of bacteria to warm milk. The bacteria feed on the sugar in milk and change it into an acid. The acid makes yogurt thick and gives it flavor.

Some companies heat yogurt after the bacteria do their job. The heat kills the bacteria. Other companies do not heat their yogurt. How can you tell which yogurts have live bacteria? Just look at the labels.

Natural **bio yogurt.**
This bio yogurt contains the following live cultures, lactobacillus bulgaricus, bifidobacterium, streptococcus thermophilus.

Yogurt with live bacteria might help people stay healthy, according to some scientists. They say it could make the immune system stronger. It might fight heart disease and some kinds of cancer. These scientists are doing tests to learn more.

The label of a yogurt container will tell you if it has live bacteria or not.

Yogurt is the only food with live bacteria. But many other foods are made with microbes. We use bacteria to make milk into cheese and sour cream. Bacteria change cabbage into sauerkraut. They turn cucumbers into pickles. They even change beef into sausage or bologna.

Food companies add bacteria to corn sugar to make xanthan gum. Xanthan gum stops ice from forming in ice cream. It also thickens salad dressing.

You've eaten foods made with other types of microbes, such as fungi. Mold is a kind of fungus. It gives blue cheese its special flavor. Yeast is a fungus too. As yeast feeds on flour, it releases a gas that makes bread light and fluffy.

Do you like chocolate? Then you should thank yeast and bacteria. In just a few days, they change bitter cocoa seeds into the rich, creamy flavor in candy bars and brownies. Thank goodness for microbes!

GLOSSARY

allergic: being very sensitive to a material that enters the body. People can be allergic to foods, pollen, skin cells shed by pets, dust mite pellets, and other substances. An allergic reaction could include itchy eyes, runny nose, wheezing, skin rash, or diarrhea.

antibiotic: a medicine that kills bacteria and other microbes. Many antibiotics are made from fungi.

bacteria: the plural form of bacterium, a tiny, one-celled living thing that reproduces by dividing

cholesterol: a substance in the body. It is needed to coat nerve cells and clean poisons out of the blood, but too much cholesterol can block blood vessels and cause heart disease.

fungus: a one-celled or multicelled living thing. Its body is made of thin threads that absorb nutrients. The plural form is fungi.

germ: a tiny organism or particle that can make you sick

gravity: a force that pulls objects toward the center of Earth or toward another large body

immune system: the group of organs, tissues, and cells that defend your body against germs and other invaders

microbe: a tiny living thing. Bacteria, protozoa, and fungi are microbes.

mite: a small, eight-legged creature related to spiders and ticks. Mites live in all kinds of places, including on the human body.

mucus: a slimy mixture that coats many surfaces inside the body. In the nose and other organs of the respiratory system, it stops germs, dirt, pollen, and other foreign particles from getting farther into the body.

nutrient: a substance that keeps the body healthy. It comes from food.

predator: an animal that hunts and kills other animals for food

prey: an animal that is hunted by a predator

protozoa: the plural of protozoan, a one-celled living thing that can move on its own and feeds on even smaller creatures

resistant: standing up to. A resistant bacterium stands up to an antibiotic. That means the bacterium cannot be harmed by the antibiotic.

saliva: a watery liquid in your mouth. It is also called spit. Saliva contains chemicals that break down food and destroy some harmful bacteria.

scabies: an itchy rash caused by female itch mites

tap water: water that comes out of a faucet

virus: a tiny particle that can make you sick. Viruses invade the cells of living things and force them to produce new viruses.

SELECTED BIBLIOGRAPHY

Bailey, Stephanie. "Bugfood II: Insects as Food." University of Kentucky Department of Entomology. January 20, 1999. http://www.uky.edu/Ag/Entomology/ythfacts/bugfood/bugfood2.htm (January 15, 2009).

Boyles, Salynn. "Plain Soap as Good as Antibacterial." WebMD. August 17, 2007. http://www.webmd.com/news/20070817/plain-soap-as-good-as-antibacterial?src=RSS_PUBLIC (January 9, 2009).

Farrell, Jeanette. *Invisible Allies: Microbes That Shape Our Lives.* New York: Farrar, Straus, and Giroux, 2005.

Latta, Sara L. *The Good, the Bad, and the Slimy: The Secret Life of Microbes.* Berkeley Heights, NJ: Enslow Publishers, 2006.

Maczulak, Anne E. *The Five-Second Rule and Other Myths about Germs.* New York: Thunder's Mouth Press, 2007.

McCloud, Linda M. "Some Simple Steps to Stop the Spread of Bacteria in Your Kitchen." Associated Press. April 23, 2007. http://www.associatedcontent.com/article/199964/some_simple_steps_to_stop_the_spread.html (January 9, 2009).

Science Daily. "Viruses Found to Spread Far and Wide as We Breathe." May 16, 2007. http://www.sciencedaily.com/releases/2007/05/070515100204.htm (January 8, 2009).

Stewart, Melissa. *Cell Biology.* Minneapolis: Twenty-First Century Books, 2008.

FURTHER READING

Jango-Cohen, Judith. *The Respiratory System.* Minneapolis: Lerner Publications Company, 2005. Jango-Cohen describes the organs of the respiratory system and explains how they work.

Larsen, C.S. *Crust & Spray: Gross Stuff in Your Eyes, Ears, Nose, and Throat.* Minneapolis: Millbrook Press, 2010. In this fun—and gross!—selection, Larsen explains what happens when harmful germs make their way into different parts of your body.

Simon, Seymour. *Guts: Our Digestive System.* New York: HarperCollins, 2005. Clearly written text, engaging full-page images, and easy-to-understand diagrams explain the human digestive system.

Siy, Alexandra, and Dennis Kunkel. *Sneeze!* Watertown, MA: Charlesbridge, 2007. Nine kids discover nine different reasons for sneezing—from dust mites to bright light and viruses. Incredible close-up photos magnify the tiny sneeze-inducing irritants.

That Explains It!
http://www.coolquiz.com/trivia/explain
The site presents all kinds of information about the human body, animals, food, inventions, machines, and more.

What Are Germs?
http://kidshealth.org/kid/talk/qa/germs.html
The site has answers for almost any question you might have about germs and how to keep your body healthy.

INDEX

ACKNOWLEDGMENTS
The images in this book are used with the permission of: © Eye
of Science/Photo Researchers, Inc., p. 1; © Nagel Photography/
Shutterstock Images, pp. 2 (top), 5; © Dr. Dennis Kunkel
Microscopy, Inc./Visuals Unlimited, Inc., pp. 2 (middle), 4,
(bottom), 10–11, 13 (top), 20, 28–29; © Liu Jixing/Shutterstock
Images, pp. 2 (bottom), 19 (inset); © jmatzick/Shutterstock
Images, pp. 3 (top), 23 (bottom right); © Jason Lugo/
iStockphoto.com, pp. 3 (bottom), 30; © Quang Ho/Shutterstock
Images, p. 4 (top); © Andrew Syred/Photo Researchers, Inc.,
pp. 6–7; © Thomas Marent/Visuals Unlimited, Inc., p. 7 (inset);
© Ian West/Bubbles Photolibrary/Alamy, p. 8; © David Phillips/
Visuals Unlimited, Inc., p. 9; © Somos Images/Alamy, p. 12;
© Yobro10/Dreamstime.com, p. 13 (bottom); © mammamaart/
iStockphoto.com, pp. 14–15; © Margoe Edwards/Shutterstock
Images, p. 16; © Ilya Andriyanov/Shutterstock Images, p. 17
(top); Centers for Disease Control and Prevention Public Health
Image Library/Dawn Arlotta, p. 17 (bottom); © Rui Saraiva/
Shutterstock Images, pp. 18–19; AP Photo/Koji Sasahara, p. 18
(inset); © Kheng Guan Toh/Shutterstock Images, p. 21; © Gerald
Bernard/Shutterstock Images, p. 22; © Rick Poley/Visuals
Unlimited, Inc., p. 23 (top); © filonmar/iStockphoto.com, p. 23
(bottom left); © Barry Rice/Visuals Unlimited, Inc., p. 24; © Mark
Handcox/Alamy, p. 25 (top); Library of Congress, LC-B8171-
0491, p. 25 (bottom); © U.H. Mayer/doc-stoc/Visuals Unlimited,
Inc., p. 26; © Photoshot, p. 27; © Betacam-SP/Shutterstock
Images, p. 29 (inset top); © Galina Barskaya/iStockphoto.com,
p. 29 (inset bottom); © TommL/iStockphoto.com, p. 31 (top);
© Todd Strand/Independent Picture Service, p. 31 (bottom);
© Image Source/Getty Images, p. 32; © Paul Cowan/
Shutterstock Images, p. 33 (top); © bronswerk/iStockphoto.
com, p. 33 (bottom); © Ray Massey/Stone/Getty Images, p. 34;
© Danny Smythe/iStockphoto.com, p. 35 (left); © Mona Lisa
Productions/Oxford Scientific/Photolibrary, p. 35 (right);
© Patrick Neri/Photolibrary, pp. 36–37; © Libby Welch/Alamy,
p. 37 (inset top left); © Wellford Tiller/iStockphoto.com, p. 37
(inset top right); © William Reavell/StockFoodCreative/Getty
Images, p. 37 (inset bottom).

Front cover: © Eye of Science/Photo Researchers, Inc. (top);
© Jacek Chabraszewski/Shutterstock Images (bottom).

Lerner Publications Company
A division of Lerner Publishing Group, Inc.
241 First Avenue North
Minneapolis, MN 55401 U.S.A.

Website address: www.lernerbooks.com

Library of Congress Cataloging-in-Publication Data

Stewart, Melissa.
    Do people really have tiny insects living in their eye-
lashes? : and other questions about the microscopic world /
Melissa Stewart.
    p.   cm. — (Is that a fact?)
    Includes bibliographical references and index.
    ISBN 978–0–7613–4916–7 (lib. bdg. : alk. paper)
    1. Microorganisms—Juvenile literature 2. Bacteria—
Juvenile literature 3. Microscopy—Juvenile literature I.
Title.
QR57.S746 2011
579—dc22   2009050431

Manufactured in the United States of America
1 – CG – 7/15/10